Division Activities

Grade 3

Written by Eliza Berkowitz

Illustrations by Clive Scruton

New York

This book belongs to

_____

New York

An Imprint of Sterling Publishing
387 Park Avenue South
New York, NY 10016

FLASH KIDS, STERLING, and the distinctive Sterling logo are registered trademarks of
Sterling Publishing Co., Inc.

Text and illustrations © 2006 by Flash Kids

Cover design and production by Mada Design, Inc.

ISBN 978-1-4114-3443-1

Distributed in Canada by Sterling Publishing
c/o Canadian Manda Group, 165 Dufferin Street
Toronto, Ontario, Canada M6K 3H6
Distributed in the United Kingdom by GMC Distribution Services
Castle Place, 166 High Street, Lewes, East Sussex, England BN7 1XU
Distributed in Australia by Capricorn Link (Australia) Pty. Ltd.
P.O. Box 704, Windsor, NSW 2756, Australia

For information about custom editions, special sales, and premium and
corporate purchases, please contact Sterling Special Sales
at 800-805-5489 or specialsales@sterlingpublishing.com.

Manufactured in China

Lot #:
4 6 8 10 9 7 5 3
03/12

www.flashkids.com

Dear Parent,

Learning to divide is an important step in your child's educational development. Dividing is a skill that your child will use later on in everyday life. This book will help your child learn the basics of division, giving him or her a strong foundation of math skills to build on. Follow these simple steps to make the most of this workbook:

- Find a comfortable place where you and your child can work quietly together.
- Encourage your child to go at his or her own pace.
- Help your child with the problems if he or she needs it.
- Offer lots of praise and support.
- Let your child reward his or her work with the included stickers.
- Most of all, remember that learning should be fun! Take time to look at the pictures, laugh at the funny characters, and enjoy this special time spent together.

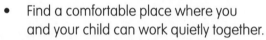

Learning Division

Division is like subtraction.

Division is a different way of taking away from a larger number.

There are different ways to show the same equation.

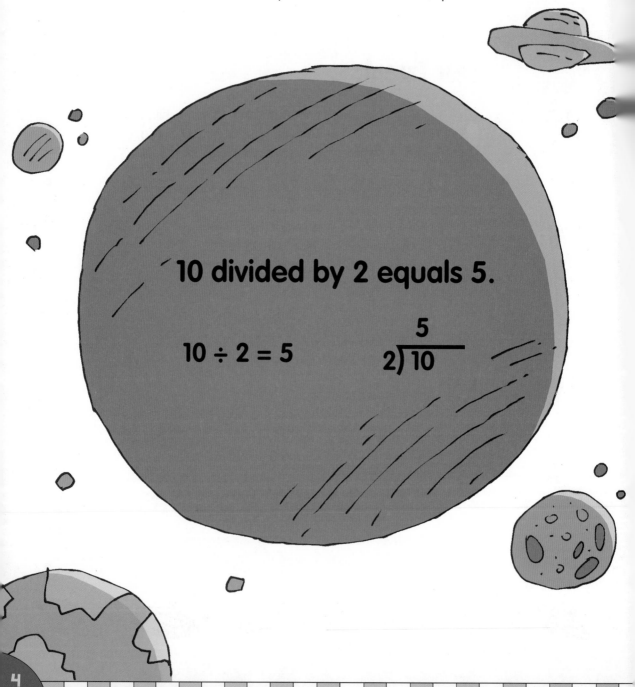

10 divided by 2 equals 5.

$$10 \div 2 = 5$$

$$2\overline{)10}^{\,5}$$

Practice Makes Perfect

To divide, you repeatedly subtract one number from a larger number. To divide 10 by 2, you subtract 2 from 10 until you cannot subtract any more. By figuring out how many times you can subtract 2 from 10, you find out what 10 divided by 2 is.

$$10 - 2 = 8$$
$$8 - 2 = 6$$
$$6 - 2 = 4$$
$$4 - 2 = 2$$
$$2 - 2 = 0$$

1. How many times could you subtract 2 from 10? _____

2. What is $10 \div 2$? _____

Dare to Divide

When you divide, you're breaking a larger
number into groups of smaller numbers.

1. There are 20 planets. Circle each group of 4.

    How many groups of 4 can you make out of 20? _____

    What is $4\overline{)20}$?

2. There are 24 space ships. Circle each group of 6.

    How many groups of 6 can you make out of 24? _____

    What is $6\overline{)24}$?

3. There are 15 planets. Circle each group of 5.

    How many groups of 5 can you make out of 15? _____

    What is $5\overline{)15}$?

Shoot for the Stars

Draw circles around groups of stars to solve the problems.

1. Count the stars.

   Draw circles around groups of 3 stars.

   How many groups of 3 are there? _____

   What is $3\overline{)9}$?

2. Count the stars.

   Draw circles around groups of 5 stars.

   How many groups of 5 are there? _____

   What is $5\overline{)15}$?

3. Count the stars.

   Draw circles around groups of 3 stars.

   How many groups of 3 are there? _____

   What is $3\overline{)12}$?

The Zero Zone

Dividing 0 by any number always gives an answer of 0. Solve the problems.

1. $3\overline{)0}$ 2. $8\overline{)0}$ 3. $4\overline{)0}$

4. $6\overline{)0}$ 5. $1\overline{)0}$ 6. $5\overline{)0}$

7. $0 \div 5 = \underline{\quad}$ 8. $0 \div 4 = \underline{\quad}$ 9. $0 \div 9 = \underline{\quad}$

10. $0 \div 8 = \underline{\quad}$ 11. $0 \div 2 = \underline{\quad}$ 12. $0 \div 20 = \underline{\quad}$

13. Your answers on page 8 should all have been the same. What was the answer? _____

14. When you divide 0 by any number you get the same answer. What is the answer? _____

Fun with One

Any number divided by one equals that number. Solve the problems.

1. $1\overline{)5}$

2. $1\overline{)7}$

3. $1\overline{)6}$

4. $1\overline{)11}$

5. $1\overline{)8}$

6. $1\overline{)3}$

7. $1\overline{)9}$

8. $1\overline{)7}$

9. $1\overline{)4}$

10. $1\overline{)2}$

11. $1\overline{)10}$

12. $1\overline{)1}$

13. $5 \div 1 =$ ___

14. $3 \div 1 =$ ___

15. $10 \div 1 =$ ___

16. $9 \div 1 =$ ___

17. $8 \div 1 =$ ___

18. $6 \div 1 =$ ___

19. $2 \div 1 =$ ___

20. $11 \div 1 =$ ___

21. $7 \div 1 =$ ___

22. $1 \div 1 =$ ___

23. $4 \div 1 =$ ___

24. $12 \div 1 =$ ___

A Dandy Dance

Solve the problems.

1. $2\overline{)4}$

2. $2\overline{)6}$

3. $4\overline{)8}$

4. $3\overline{)3}$

5. $2\overline{)10}$

6. $2\overline{)12}$

7. $2\overline{)8}$

8. $1\overline{)9}$

9. $4\overline{)12}$

10. $2\overline{)2}$

11. $3\overline{)12}$

12. $2\overline{)10}$

A Pretty Pet

Solve the problems.

1. 4)8   2. 1)8   3. 2)6   4. 3)3

5. 1)6   6. 2)8   7. 4)16   8. 1)5

9. 3)15   10. 2)16   11. 2)12   12. 3)9

Blast Off!

Solve the problems.

1. 2)10

2. 1)7

3. 4)12

4. 5)10

5. 3)12

6. 5)15

7. 2)18

8. 3)15

9. 5)20

10. 4)24

11. 1)9

12. 2)16

Basketball for All

Solve the problems.

1. $3\overline{)15}$ 2. $2\overline{)12}$ 3. $7\overline{)14}$ 4. $5\overline{)20}$

5. $2\overline{)16}$ 6. $7\overline{)21}$ 7. $5\overline{)25}$ 8. $2\overline{)10}$

9. $7\overline{)14}$ 10. $3\overline{)18}$

11. $1\overline{)6}$

12. $2\overline{)18}$

Fun with Family

Solve the problems.

1. $6\overline{)18}$ 2. $3\overline{)12}$ 3. $5\overline{)20}$ 4. $4\overline{)16}$

5. $7\overline{)14}$ 6. $4\overline{)20}$ 7. $4\overline{)24}$ 8. $7\overline{)28}$

9. $6\overline{)12}$ 10. $3\overline{)15}$ 11. $5\overline{)30}$ 12. $4\overline{)12}$

Meals in Space

Solve the problems.

1. $5\overline{)20}$

2. $4\overline{)24}$

3. $8\overline{)16}$

4. $3\overline{)18}$

5. $5\overline{)25}$

6. $2\overline{)18}$

7. $6\overline{)24}$

8. $4\overline{)20}$

9. $3\overline{)27}$

10. $5\overline{)20}$

11. $7\overline{)21}$

12. $2\overline{)10}$

Jolly Jump Rope

Solve the problems.

1. 2)10

2. 7)14

3. 5)25

4. 8)24

5. 9)18

6. 3)21

7. 6)18

8. 5)15

9. 3)27

10. 8)16

11. 4)16

12. 7)35

A Lot of Lollipops!

Solve the problems.

1. $24 \div 6 =$ _____

2. $27 \div 3 =$ _____

3. $35 \div 7 =$ _____

4. $12 \div 2 =$ _____

5. $20 \div 4 =$ _____

6. $24 \div 3 =$ _____

7. $16 \div 4 =$ _____

8. $12 \div 6 =$ _____

9. $28 \div 4 =$ _____

10. $28 \div 7 =$ _____

11. $20 \div 5 =$ _____

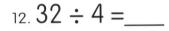

12. $32 \div 4 =$ _____

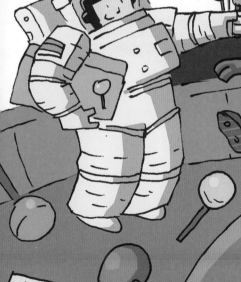

Fruits and Veggies

1. Benny has 12 apples. He puts them in groups of 3.

   How many groups of apples does he have? _____

2. Sarah has 24 carrots. She puts them in stacks of 8.

   How many stacks of carrots does she have? _____

3. Rebecca has 18 strawberries. She puts them in piles of 3.

   How many piles of strawberries does she have? _____

Candy Time!

1. Davie gives 4 lollipops to each alien he meets. He gives away 24 lollipops. How many aliens did he meet? _____

2. Roger gives 3 candy bars to each alien he meets. He gives away 15 candy bars. How many aliens did he meet? _____

3. Joanne gives 4 bits of chocolate to each alien she meets. She gives away 16 bits of chocolate. How many aliens did she meet? _____

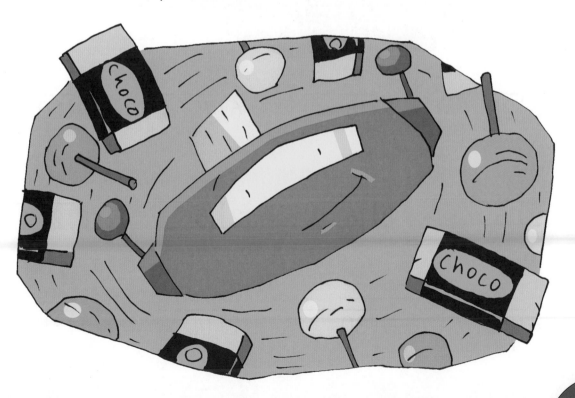

A Great Game

Solve the problems.

1. 5)25

2. 2)18

3. 6)42

4. 4)20

5. 2)16

6. 8)16

7. 2)10

8. 8)24

9. 4)24

10. 5)30

11. 2)14

12. 7)21

Super Stars

Solve the problems.

1. $4\overline{)24}$ 2. $9\overline{)27}$ 3. $5\overline{)25}$ 4. $3\overline{)24}$

5. $6\overline{)18}$ 6. $7\overline{)14}$ 7. $6\overline{)24}$ 8. $3\overline{)27}$

9. $7\overline{)28}$ 10. $4\overline{)32}$ 11. $9\overline{)54}$ 12. $8\overline{)40}$

Say Yes to Chess!

Solve the problems.

1. 5)30

2. 4)16

3. 7)21

4. 6)24

5. 1)10

6. 2)2

7. 3)12

8. 4)28

9. 5)25

10. 8)32

11. 7)14

12. 2)14

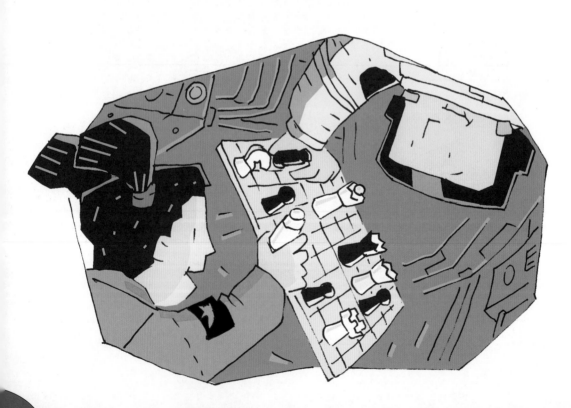

Fun on the Moon

Solve the problems.

1. $3\overline{)27}$

2. $4\overline{)20}$

3. $9\overline{)36}$

4. $6\overline{)36}$

5. $3\overline{)3}$

6. $7\overline{)28}$

7. $3\overline{)3}$

8. $8\overline{)24}$

9. $9\overline{)45}$

10. $3\overline{)12}$

11. $7\overline{)21}$

12. $6\overline{)30}$

Games of Tennis

1. Matty has 12 tennis balls. If 3 balls fit in a can, how many cans can he fill with tennis balls? _____

2. Jules has 25 tennis racquets. If he separates them into groups of 5, how many groups will he have? _____

3. Matty and Jules play a tennis match for 56 minutes. If they played 7 sets of equal length, how many minutes long was each set? _____

4. Joanne has 27 tennis balls. If 3 balls fit in a can, how many cans can she fill with tennis balls? _____

5. Mark has 25 tennis racquets. If he separates them into groups of 5, how many groups will he have? _____

6. Joanne and Mark play a tennis match for 27 minutes. If they played 9 sets of equal length, how many minutes long was each set? _____

A Silly Story

Solve the problems.

1. $4\overline{)24}$

2. $7\overline{)35}$

3. $2\overline{)12}$

4. $9\overline{)45}$

5. $3\overline{)27}$

6. $5\overline{)30}$

7. $1\overline{)7}$

8. $4\overline{)28}$

9. $9\overline{)27}$

10. $5\overline{)25}$

11. $6\overline{)18}$

12. $4\overline{)36}$

Riding Bikes

Solve the problems.

1. $6\overline{)36}$ 2. $3\overline{)24}$ 3. $1\overline{)5}$ 4. $5\overline{)15}$

5. $8\overline{)32}$ 6. $2\overline{)14}$ 7. $7\overline{)14}$ 8. $2\overline{)6}$

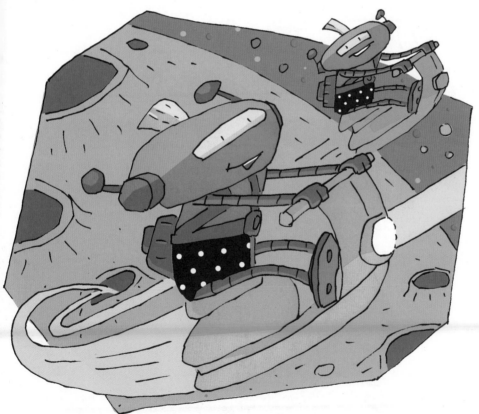

9. $3\overline{)24}$

10. $4\overline{)36}$

11. $8\overline{)16}$

12. $7\overline{)28}$

A Ton of Tunes

Solve the problems.

1. $6\overline{)30}$　　2. $9\overline{)45}$　　3. $7\overline{)49}$　　4. $3\overline{)24}$

5. $9\overline{)54}$　　6. $2\overline{)14}$　　7. $9\overline{)18}$　　8. $6\overline{)36}$

9. $5\overline{)25}$　　10. $7\overline{)42}$

11. $2\overline{)18}$

12. $4\overline{)16}$

A Wonderful Wedding

Solve the problems.

1. $5\overline{)35}$

2. $7\overline{)56}$

3. $2\overline{)2}$

4. $6\overline{)42}$

5. $4\overline{)0}$

6. $8\overline{)64}$

7. $1\overline{)9}$

8. $9\overline{)72}$

9. $5\overline{)30}$

10. $9\overline{)27}$

11. $7\overline{)35}$

12. $6\overline{)48}$

A Picnic in the Park

1. Ronnie cooks the same number of meals each day. She cooks 27 meals in 9 days. How many meals does she cook each day? _____

2. Barbara eats 18 carrots in 3 days. If she eats the same number of carrots each day, how many carrots does she eat each day? _____

3. Ralph drinks the same amount of milk every day. He drinks 36 glasses of milk in 4 days. How many glasses of milk does he drink each day? _____

4. Debbie drinks the same amount of soda every day. She drinks 36 cans of soda in 6 days. How many cans of soda does she drink each day? _____

5. Ronald eats 45 apples in 9 days. How many apples does he eat each day, if he eats the same number of apples each day? _____

6. Artie eats 27 peanut butter sandwiches in 9 days. If he eats the same number of sandwiches every day, how many peanut butter sandwiches does he eat each day? _____

Painting a Picture

Solve the problems.

1. $5\overline{)35}$ 2. $6\overline{)54}$ 3. $1\overline{)1}$ 4. $4\overline{)24}$

5. $7\overline{)28}$ 6. $5\overline{)5}$ 7. $2\overline{)16}$ 8. $5\overline{)45}$

9. $9\overline{)27}$ 10. $8\overline{)48}$ 11. $4\overline{)36}$ 12. $1\overline{)9}$

Looking Up

Solve the problems.

1. $7\overline{)49}$ 2. $4\overline{)36}$ 3. $5\overline{)45}$ 4. $8\overline{)64}$

5. $4\overline{)28}$ 6. $4\overline{)20}$ 7. $6\overline{)30}$ 8. $5\overline{)15}$

9. $4\overline{)8}$ 10. $9\overline{)18}$ 11. $6\overline{)24}$ 12. $5\overline{)30}$

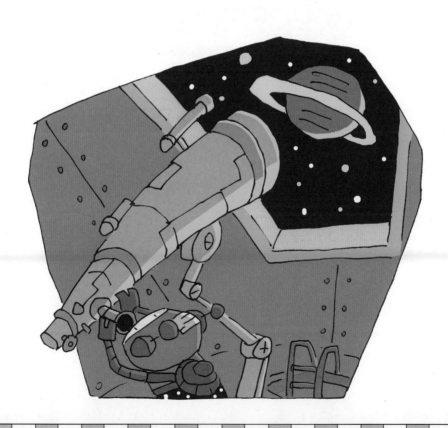

Magical Music

Solve the problems.

1. $7\overline{)28}$ 2. $9\overline{)36}$ 3. $8\overline{)72}$ 4. $5\overline{)40}$

5. $7\overline{)35}$ 6. $3\overline{)27}$ 7. $7\overline{)21}$ 8. $3\overline{)9}$

9. $8\overline{)24}$ 10. $7\overline{)49}$ 11. $9\overline{)45}$ 12. $4\overline{)12}$

Shopping in Space

Solve the problems.

1. $6\overline{)42}$ 2. $8\overline{)24}$ 3. $3\overline{)3}$ 4. $9\overline{)9}$

5. $6\overline{)30}$ 6. $4\overline{)16}$ 7. $8\overline{)32}$ 8. $6\overline{)36}$

9. $9\overline{)27}$ 10. $8\overline{)72}$

11. $7\overline{)49}$

12. $6\overline{)12}$

A Crazy Classroom

1. Bobby used 45 pencils in 9 days. He used the same number of pencils each day. How many pencils did he use each day? _____

2. Fran raised her hand the same number of times each day. She raised her hand 25 times in 5 days. How many times did she raise her hand each day? _____

3. Rita used 6 sheets of paper to write 36 paragraphs. How many paragraphs did she write on each piece of paper? _____

4. Mrs. Locker got 40 apples from her students in 5 days. She got the same number of apples each day. How many apples did she get each day? _____

5. Darren put 24 erasers into groups of 3 on his desk. How many groups of erasers did he have? _____

6. Tony asked 54 questions in 6 days. He asked the same number of questions each day. How many questions did he ask each day? _____

A Deep Sleep

Solve the problems.

1. $6\overline{)42}$ 2. $7\overline{)49}$ 3. $7\overline{)0}$ 4. $9\overline{)18}$

5. $9\overline{)81}$ 6. $4\overline{)32}$ 7. $7\overline{)21}$ 8. $9\overline{)63}$

9. $4\overline{)16}$

10. $5\overline{)35}$

11. $6\overline{)36}$

12. $8\overline{)40}$

Clowning Around

Solve the problems.

1. $5\overline{)25}$ 2. $8\overline{)64}$ 3. $3\overline{)12}$ 4. $5\overline{)40}$

5. $4\overline{)36}$ 6. $8\overline{)24}$ 7. $3\overline{)3}$ 8. $7\overline{)28}$

9. $6\overline{)18}$ 10. $3\overline{)9}$ 11. $8\overline{)72}$ 12. $7\overline{)56}$

Love Up Above

Solve the problems.

1. $5\overline{)25}$ 　　 2. $3\overline{)18}$ 　　 3. $4\overline{)16}$ 　　 4. $1\overline{)7}$

5. $7\overline{)63}$ 　　 6. $9\overline{)36}$ 　　 7. $6\overline{)24}$ 　　 8. $9\overline{)27}$

9. $3\overline{)24}$ 　　 10. $5\overline{)25}$ 　　 11. $4\overline{)36}$ 　　 12. $7\overline{)63}$

A Call for Football

Solve the problems.

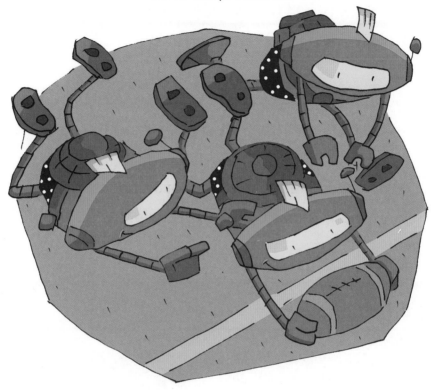

1. $5\overline{)45}$ 2. $6\overline{)30}$ 3. $9\overline{)36}$ 4. $4\overline{)16}$

5. $7\overline{)28}$ 6. $9\overline{)81}$ 7. $7\overline{)49}$ 8. $8\overline{)64}$

9. $5\overline{)40}$ 10. $6\overline{)42}$ 11. $8\overline{)24}$ 12. $6\overline{)48}$

Bookworm Buddies

1. Matthew put 24 books into 3 equal stacks. How many books were in each stack? _____

2. Darla put 36 books into 6 equal groups. How many books did she put in each group? _____

3. Ryan made 4 equal piles out of 32 books. How many books were in each pile? _____

4. Cara put 25 books into 5 equal stacks.

   How many books were in each stack? _____

5. James put 18 books into 3 equal groups.

   How many books were in each group? _____

6. Margie made 4 equal piles out of 16 books.

   How many books were in each pile? _____

At the Carnival

Solve the problems.

1. 5)35

2. 7)21

3. 9)81

4. 6)42

5. 6)18

6. 7)14

7. 7)28

8. 3)27

9. 6)36

10. 9)45

11. 8)8

12. 7)63

Meet and Greet

Solve the problems.

1. $8\overline{)32}$ 2. $9\overline{)45}$ 3. $3\overline{)9}$ 4. $2\overline{)14}$

5. $5\overline{)40}$ 6. $6\overline{)54}$ 7. $7\overline{)21}$ 8. $2\overline{)12}$

9. $9\overline{)81}$ 10. $4\overline{)28}$ 11. $6\overline{)48}$ 12. $5\overline{)45}$

Seeing Stars

Solve the problems. Begin by dividing the number in the tens place, then move to the ones place.

1. $2\overline{)20}$

2. $4\overline{)40}$

3. $9\overline{)90}$

4. $6\overline{)60}$

5. $1\overline{)10}$

6. $7\overline{)70}$

7. $3\overline{)30}$

8. $8\overline{)80}$

Solve the problems. Begin by dividing the number in the hundreds place, then move to the tens place and the ones place.

9. $4\overline{)400}$

10. $6\overline{)600}$

11. $3\overline{)300}$

12. $7\overline{)700}$

13. $9\overline{)900}$

14. $2\overline{)200}$

15. $5\overline{)500}$

$8\overline{)800}$

Getting Around in Space

Solve the problems.

1. 5)45

2. 9)81

3. 6)60

4. 4)400

5. 9)90

6. 6)42

7. 8)80

8. 7)28

9. 5)25

10. 3)300

11. 9)45

Hooray for Hopscotch!

Solve the problems.

1. 7)56

2. 6)42

3. 8)64

4. 1)25

5. 6)48

6. 4)24

7. 5)500

8. 2)20

9. 3)30

10. 7)70

11. 9)27

12. 4)400

Happy Birthday!

1. Ali got 24 gifts from 8 people at her birthday party. Everyone got her the same number of gifts. How many gifts did each person give her? _____

2. At the party, 8 people ate 16 slices of birthday cake. Each person had the same amount of cake. How many slices of cake did each person eat? _____

3. They played games at the party for 80 minutes. They played 8 games for an equal amount of time. How many games did they play? _____

4. Ali had 9 people at her party. They came to the party in 3 cars. Each car had the same number of kids. How many kids came in each car? _____

5. At the party, 4 kids ate 16 hot dogs. The kids ate an equal number of hot dogs. How many hot dogs did they each eat? _____

6. Ali gave out 90 prizes at her party. The 9 kids at the party got an equal number of prizes. How many did they each get? _____

In the Shade

Solve the problems. Begin by dividing the number in the hundreds place, then move to the tens place and the ones place. If the number in the hundreds place is too small, try dividing the numbers in both the hundreds and tens place as one number.

1. 4)444

2. 6)660

3. 5)255

4. 2)482

5. 9)189

6. 3)690

7. 6)246

8. 7)357

9. 5)505

10. 8)328

11. 4)164

12. 8)488

Riding a Rollercoaster

Solve the problems.

1. $7\overline{)497}$ 2. $2\overline{)242}$ 3. $9\overline{)819}$ 4. $7\overline{)770}$

5. $4\overline{)364}$ 6. $6\overline{)366}$ 7. $3\overline{)183}$ 8. $5\overline{)405}$

9. $8\overline{)328}$

10. $2\overline{)868}$

11. $9\overline{)459}$

12. $7\overline{)350}$

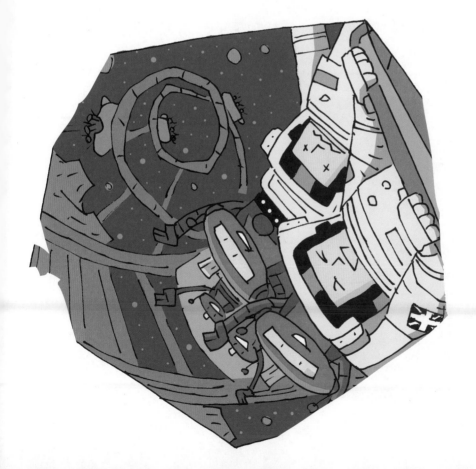

Three Little Aliens

Solve the problems.

1. 6)420

2. 8)168

3. 5)155

4. 7)217

5. 4)248

6. 9)369

7. 2)684

8. 5)355

9. 3)693

10. 7)497

11. 8)648

12. 6)126

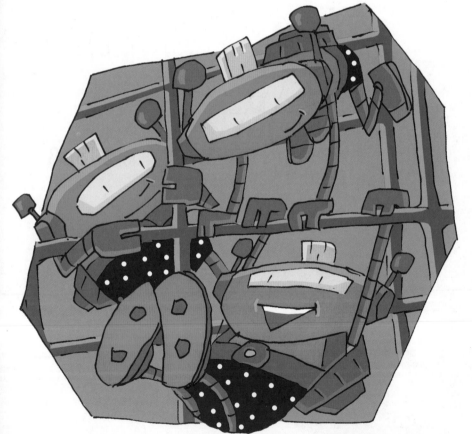

On the Beach

Solve the problems.

1. 7)770

2. 3)936

3. 6)180

4. 4)324

5. 9)270

6. 3)633

7. 7)497

8. 4)160

9. 2)128

10. 7)217

11. 6)426

12. 8)640

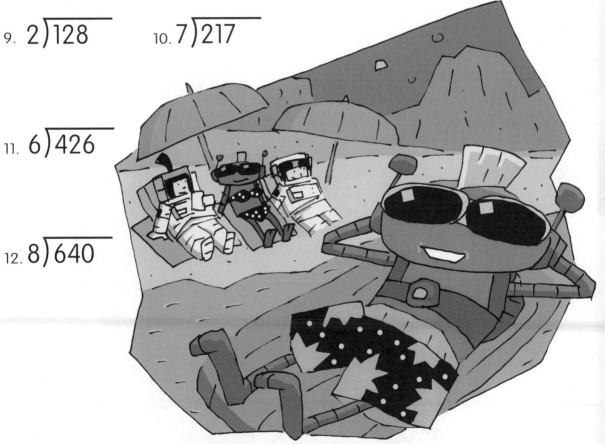

Parade in the Park

Solve the problems. Begin by dividing the number in the thousands place, then move to the hundreds place, then the tens place, and then the ones place. If the number in the thousands place is too small, try dividing the numbers in both the thousands and hundreds place as one number.

1. $3\overline{)6963}$ 2. $4\overline{)8448}$ 3. $2\overline{)6842}$ 4. $3\overline{)9963}$

5. $4\overline{)4880}$ 6. $3\overline{)3990}$ 7. $4\overline{)4480}$ 8. $2\overline{)2684}$

9. $4\overline{)4408}$ 10. $3\overline{)3669}$ 11. $2\overline{)2448}$ 12. $2\overline{)4206}$

Alien Aquarium

Solve the problems.

1. 5)1055

2. 6)1860

3. 8)2480

4. 4)8804

5. 2)6020

6. 3)9033

7. 5)5550

8. 6)1266

9. 7)4977

10. 3)6906

11. 3)2133

12. 2)8044

Faraway Friends

Solve the problems.

1. $8\overline{)8088}$ 2. $7\overline{)4977}$ 3. $3\overline{)6903}$ 4. $4\overline{)4408}$

5. $8\overline{)6488}$ 6. $5\overline{)2500}$ 7. $7\overline{)6377}$ 8. $8\overline{)3280}$

9. $2\overline{)8240}$ 10. $6\overline{)3660}$ 11. $3\overline{)9366}$ 12. $5\overline{)5055}$

Astronaut Adventure

Solve the problems.

1. $9\overline{)9090}$
2. $4\overline{)1640}$
3. $6\overline{)1266}$
4. $5\overline{)4050}$

5. $2\overline{)2864}$
6. $3\overline{)9960}$
7. $8\overline{)6488}$
8. $6\overline{)1860}$

9. $7\overline{)2177}$
10. $9\overline{)1899}$
11. $7\overline{)4900}$

Answer Key

Page 5
1. 5
2. 5

Page 6
1. 5
2. 4
3. 3

Page 7
1. 3
2. 3
3. 4

Pages 8 and 9
1. 0   8. 0
2. 0   9. 0
3. 0   10. 0
4. 0   11. 0
5. 0   12. 0
6. 0   13. 0
7. 0   14. 0

Pages 10 and 11
1. 5   13. 5
2. 7   14. 3
3. 6   15. 10
4. 11   16. 9
5. 8   17. 8
6. 3   18. 6
7. 9   19. 2
8. 7   20. 11
9. 4   21. 7
10. 2   22. 1
11. 10 23. 4
12. 1   24. 12

Page 12
1. 2   7. 4
2. 3   8. 9
3. 2   9. 3
4. 1   10. 1
5. 5   11. 4
6. 6   12. 5

Page 13
1. 2   7. 4
2. 8   8. 5
3. 3   9. 5
4. 1   10. 8
5. 6   11. 6
6. 4   12. 3

Page 14
1. 5   7. 9
2. 7   8. 5
3. 3   9. 4
4. 2   10. 6
5. 4   11. 9
6. 3   12. 8

Page 15
1. 5   7. 5
2. 6   8. 5
3. 2   9. 2
4. 4   10. 6
5. 8   11. 6
6. 3   12. 9

Page 16
1. 3   7. 6
2. 4   8. 4
3. 4   9. 2
4. 4   10. 5
5. 2   11. 6
6. 5   12. 3

Page 17
1. 4   7. 4
2. 6   8. 5
3. 2   9. 9
4. 6   10. 4
5. 5   11. 3
6. 9   12. 5

Page 18
1. 5   7. 3
2. 2   8. 3
3. 5   9. 9
4. 3   10. 2
5. 2   11. 4
6. 7   12. 5

Page 19
1. 4   7. 4
2. 9   8. 2
3. 5   9. 7
4. 6   10. 4
5. 5   11. 4
6. 8   12. 8

Page 20
1. 4
2. 3
3. 6

Page 21
1. 6
2. 5
3. 4

Page 22
1. 5   7. 5
2. 9   8. 3
3. 7   9. 6
4. 5   10. 6
5. 8   11. 7
6. 2   12. 3

Page 23
1. 6   7. 4
2. 3   8. 9
3. 5   9. 4
4. 8   10. 8
5. 3   11. 6
6. 2   12. 5

Page 24
1. 6   7. 4
2. 4   8. 7
3. 3   9. 5
4. 4   10. 4
5. 10   11. 2
6. 1   12. 7

Page 25
1. 9   7. 1
2. 5   8. 3
3. 4   9. 5
4. 6   10. 4
5. 1   11. 3
6. 4   12. 5

Pages 26 and 27
1. 4
2. 5
3. 8
4. 9
5. 5
6. 3

Page 28
1. 6   7. 7
2. 5   8. 7
3. 6   9. 3
4. 5   10. 5
5. 9   11. 3
6. 6   12. 9

Page 29
1. 6   7. 2
2. 8   8. 3
3. 5   9. 8
4. 3   10. 9
5. 4   11. 2
6. 7   12. 4

Page 30
1. 5   7. 2
2. 5   8. 6
3. 7   9. 5
4. 8   10. 6
5. 6   11. 9
6. 7   12. 4

Page 31
1. 7   7. 9
2. 8   8. 8
3. 1   9. 6
4. 7   10. 3
5. 0   11. 5
6. 8   12. 8

Pages 32 and 33
1. 3
2. 6
3. 9
4. 6
5. 5
6. 3

Page 34
1. 7   7. 8
2. 9   8. 9
3. 1   9. 3
4. 6   10. 6
5. 4   11. 9
6. 1   12. 9

Page 35
1. 7   7. 5
2. 9   8. 3
3. 9   9. 2
4. 8   10. 2
5. 7   11. 4
6. 5   12. 6

Page 36
1. 4   7. 3
2. 4   8. 3
3. 9   9. 3
4. 8   10. 7
5. 5   11. 5
6. 9   12. 3

Page 37
1. 7   7. 4
2. 3   8. 6
3. 1   9. 3
4. 1   10. 9
5. 5   11. 7
6. 4   12. 2

Pages 38 and 39
1. 5
2. 5
3. 6
4. 8
5. 8
6. 9

Page 40
1. 7   7. 3
2. 7   8. 7
3. 0   9. 4
4. 2   10. 7
5. 9   11. 6
6. 8   12. 5

Answer Key

Page 41
1. 5   7. 1
2. 8   8. 4
3. 4   9. 3
4. 8   10. 3
5. 9   11. 9
6. 3   12. 8

Page 42
1. 5   7. 4
2. 6   8. 3
3. 4   9. 8
4. 7   10. 5
5. 9   11. 9
6. 4   12. 9

Page 43
1. 9   7. 7
2. 5   8. 8
3. 4   9. 8
4. 4   10. 7
5. 4   11. 3
6. 9   12. 8

Pages 44 and 45
1. 8
2. 6
3. 8
4. 5
5. 6
6. 4

Page 46
1. 7   7. 4
2. 3   8. 9
3. 9   9. 6
4. 7   10. 5
5. 3   11. 1
6. 2   12. 9

Page 47
1. 4   7. 3
2. 5   8. 6
3. 3   9. 9
4. 7   10. 7
5. 8   11. 8
6. 9   12. 9

Pages 48 and 49
1. 10   9. 100
2. 10   10. 100
3. 10   11. 100
4. 10   12. 100
5. 10   13. 100
6. 10   14. 100
7. 10   15. 100
8. 10   16. 100

Page 50
1. 9   7. 10
2. 9   8. 4
3. 10   9. 5
4. 100   10. 100
5. 10   11. 5
6. 7

Page 51
1. 8   7. 100
2. 7   8. 10
3. 8   9. 10
4. 25   10. 10
5. 8   11. 3
6. 6   12. 100

Pages 52 and 53
1. 3
2. 2
3. 10
4. 3
5. 4
6. 10

Page 54
1. 111   7. 41
2. 110   8. 51
3. 51   9. 101
4. 241   10. 41
5. 21   11. 41
6. 230   12. 61

Page 55
1. 71   7. 61
2. 121   8. 81
3. 91   9. 41
4. 110   10. 434
5. 91   11. 51
6. 61   12. 50

Page 56
1. 70   7. 342
2. 21   8. 71
3. 31   9. 231
4. 31   10. 71
5. 62   11. 81
6. 41   12. 21

Page 57
1. 110   7. 71
2. 312   8. 40
3. 30   9. 64
4. 81   10. 31
5. 30   11. 71
6. 211   12. 80

Page 58
1. 2321   7. 1120
2. 2112   8. 1342
3. 3421   9. 1102
4. 3321   10. 1223
5. 1220   11. 1224
6. 1330   12. 2103

Page 59
1. 211   7. 1110
2. 310   8. 211
3. 310   9. 711
4. 2201   10. 2302
5. 3010   11. 711
6. 3011   12. 4022

Page 60
1. 1011   7. 911
2. 711   8. 410
3. 2301   9. 4120
4. 1102   10. 610
5. 811   11. 3122
6. 500   12. 1011

Page 61
1. 1010   6. 3320
2. 410   7. 811
3. 211   8. 310
4. 810   9. 311
5. 1432   10. 211
         11. 700